Death and Disease

Alex Woolf

LUCENT BOOKS®

THOMSON

GALE

San Diego • Detroit • New York • San Francisco • Cleveland • New Haven, Conn. • Waterville, Maine • London • Munich

THOMSON

GALE

© 2004 by Hodder Wayland

Originally published by Hodder Wayland,
an imprint of Hodder Children's Books,
a division of Hodder Headline Limited
338 Euston Road, London NW1 3BH

For more information, contact
Lucent Books
27500 Drake Rd.
Farmington Hills, MI 48331-3535
Or you can visit our Internet site at http://www.gale.com

Series Concept: Jane Tyler
Design: Peta Morey
Editor: Liz Gogerly
Picture Researcher: Glass Onion Pictures
Consultant: Malcolm Barber
Map artwork: Encompass

We are grateful to the following for permission to reproduce photographs: AKG, London 6, 7, 9, 10, 12, 24, 26, 28, 35, 38, 41, 42, 42, 43, 44; Art Archive 25, 29, 40; Bridgeman Art Library/ Bibliotheque Municipale, Laon, France 5 (bottom)/ Musee Conde, Chantilly, France 8, 14, 34/ Osterreichische Nationalbibliothek, Vienna, Austria 16, 17/ Private Collection 18, 21/ Bibliotheque des Arts Decoratifs, Paris, France 19/ Victoria and Albert Museum, London, UK 22/ British Library, London, UK 27/ Musee des Beaux-Arts, Marseille, France 30/ Library of Congress, Washington, USA 31/ Lambeth Palace Library, London, UK 33/ Bibliotheque Municipale, Bologne sur Mer, France 11, 36/ Musee de la Faculte de Medecine, Montpellier, France 37/ Bibliotheque Nationale, Paris, France 39, 45; British Library 13, 32; FLPA 20; Philip Sauvain 4; Topham Picturepoint 15; Trinity College Library, Cambridge 5 (top)

Cover pictures: © Archivo Iconografico, S. A./CORBIS

LIBRARY OF CONGRESS CATALOGING-IN-PUBLICATION DATA

Woolf, Alex, 1964–,
    Death and disease / Alex Woolf
        p. cm. — (Medieval realms)
Includes bibliographical references and index.
    ISBN 1-59018-533-1 (hbk.: alk. paper)
    1. Public health—history I. Title. II. Series.

RA424.W64 2004
610'.94'0902—dc22

2003061797

Printed in China

Contents

Health and Disease in 1000 A.D.

AT THE BEGINNING of the Middle Ages, in the year 1000 A.D., Europeans did not have the same expectations of good health and long life as we do today. If a person survived infancy, then on average they could expect to live into their forties or fifties, assuming that they were fortunate enough to escape death in war or in childbirth. The most common causes of death were unclean water, poor diet, and a lack of hygiene, especially in the overcrowded towns and cities. Human waste often got into the water supply, causing diseases like **typhoid** and **cholera**.

Medicine

There were very few medical schools in Europe in 1000 A.D., and medical knowledge was very poor compared to today. Doctors based their remedies on ancient theories or folklore, rather than from studying their patients. The internal workings of the body were a mystery. Both doctors and patients believed that a person's state of health depended to a large extent on the will of God. There were hospitals run by **monasteries** and **convents**, but treatment was rather basic and many people regarded hospitals as places for the dying.

Diseases

In spite of these problems, the population of Europe was actually rising in 1000 A.D. Between 950 and 1250, Europe's population rose from about 25 million to 75 million. One reason for this was that Europe had few infectious diseases during this period. The most feared disease at this time was leprosy (see pages 18–19). This disease had terrifying

In medieval times, waste was often poured from people's windows into the streets. The usual warning cry was "Gardez l'eau," French for "watch the water".

Medieval Toilets

In medieval times, there was no sewage system to carry away human waste. Sewage was just left to pile up. In the countryside, these piles—called middens—were often near villages, causing health risks. There was no indoor plumbing, and city streets had open drains, so that people could empty their "pysse" pots from their windows. In 1358, London had just four public toilets. The largest emptied straight into the River Thames.

An arrowhead is pulled out of a patient. Medieval kingdoms were often at war with each other, and surgeons became practiced at dealing with battle injuries.

symptoms, but it was not very **contagious**, and it rarely killed its victims, so had little effect on population levels.

Most diseases in 1000 A.D. affected only small areas of Europe and were not widespread. They were linked to local conditions, such as famine and bad diet. Some diseases were caught from infected plants. An example of this was ergotism, also known as St. Vitus's Disease. This was a dreadful, often fatal, illness caused by eating grain contaminated by a fungus called ergot. A chemical in ergot would make sufferers go insane, giving them the sensation of being burned alive.

The major infectious diseases of the previous thousand years had virtually disappeared by 1000 A.D. Smallpox and measles were two major diseases afflicting Europe between 250 and 500 A.D. However, by the eleventh century these were known mainly as killers of children. Even the deadly plague (see pages 20–21), which had devastated Europe between the sixth and eighth centuries, was almost unknown in Europe by the eleventh century. Life was certainly tough in 1000 A.D., but Europeans could at least count themselves fortunate that they did not suffer the deadly diseases of their ancestors.

Medieval doctors believed that certain herbs and plants had magical properties. They used them to cool fevers, take away pain, and protect people from disease.

The Legacy of the Ancient World

FOR MUCH of the medieval period, European doctors based their techniques and treatments on theories developed in the ancient world, which were later passed on to them by Arabic scholars and physicians. The two outstanding figures of ancient medicine, whose ideas dominated medieval medical practice, were both Greek. Their names were Hippocrates and Galen.

Hippocrates

Hippocrates (*c.* 460–377 B.C.) is known as the "father of medicine." He investigated a wide range of subjects, including **anatomy**, diseases, and the treatment of illness by diet and drugs. He was important not because he discovered lots of cures (many of his theories about the causes of disease were completely wrong), but because he was the first to approach medicine as a science.

> ### Avicenna (Ibn Sina) 980–1037 A.D.
>
> Hippocrates' and Galen's works were all but lost to Europe for hundreds of years. They were, however, collected and translated by Arab scholars and physicians and, by the end of the tenth century, these ancient theories were finding their way back to Europe. A Persian doctor and philosopher named Avicenna was a key figure in reintroducing Europeans to the ideas of Galen. Avicenna wrote over two hundred books, including his famous *Canon*—a medical textbook that combined Galen's theories with more recent medical discoveries. Avicenna's *Canon* was used in universities until the eighteenth century.

In this thirteenth-century illustration, an Arab physician prepares a medical treatment. Arab doctors were the first to identify diseases such as smallpox, measles, and scarlet fever.

A thirteenth-century wall painting of Galen (left) and Hippocrates. Both were determined to find the real causes of illness and disease.

In ancient times, most people believed death and disease were caused by the gods. Hippocrates argued that physicians should look for natural causes, not supernatural ones. They should observe the patient, decide what he or she was suffering from, and then offer a treatment. Hippocrates stressed the importance of a good diet, exercise, and fresh air to help the body heal itself.

Hippocrates was also the first to introduce moral standards in medicine. All his students had to follow a strict code of behavior. They swore an oath to support their fellow doctors, to keep a patient's medical problems to themselves, and never to deliberately poison a patient. To this day, newly qualified doctors can choose to swear the Hippocratic Oath.

Galen

Claudius Galen (*c.* 129–216 A.D.) was the first person to make an in-depth study of anatomy. He studied the inner workings of pigs, goats, and apes, and applied what he learned to the human body. Galen discovered, for example, that blood moved within the body (though not that it circulated), and that cutting the spinal cord caused a loss of movement in the lower body. Galen suggested the idea of using opposites to treat illnesses, for example giving patients cool liquid or food if they have a fever. He was also the first person to take a patient's pulse to help with **diagnosis**, a method that doctors still use today.

The Four Humors

The theory on which much medieval medicine was based was developed in ancient Greece in around 400 B.C., probably by Hippocrates. According to this theory, the body has four humors, or fluids—blood, phlegm, black bile and yellow bile—and if these humors lose their natural balance, a person becomes ill. Most medieval treatments were aimed at trying to restore this natural balance. It was only in the fifteenth century that the theory of the four humors began to be challenged (see page 45).

The Influence of the Church

IN MEDIEVAL TIMES, religion and medicine were closely linked because of the popular belief that God and the devil were responsible for health. Illness and disease were seen as God's punishment for people's sins, and people placed as much faith in prayer as they did in medicine. It was therefore natural that the Church, which controlled most aspects of life in the Middle Ages, should play an important role in medicine.

The Effect on Medicine

The Church was resistant to new ideas, and hindered the progress of European medicine during the first half of the Middle Ages. Church leaders were hostile to those who wished to study the workings of the human body.

In this fifteenth-century illustration, a king lies on his deathbed as a priest prays for his soul. In medieval times, people believed that God decided when someone should die, and it was beyond the power of humans to prolong life.

Miracle Cures

Many people believed that direct appeals to God or the saints could bring about miracle cures. During the early Middle Ages, shrines to saints appeared in various parts of Europe. These shrines became centers where the sick or injured, or those thought to be possessed by demons, could pray in the hope of being cured. Saints became associated with the cure of certain ailments. Saint Lucy of Syracuse (in Sicily), for example, was believed to be able to cure eye problems. Another practice that was believed to cause miracle healings was the **anointment** of a sick person with oil by a priest. This was seen as a way of purifying a person of sin.

The Christian belief in the **resurrection** of the body meant that corpses could not be cut open for study. Doctors were forced to rely on Galen's notes about the anatomy of pigs for their understanding of how the human body worked.

When the ideas of Avicenna and Galen began to reappear in Europe in the eleventh century, many **clerics** were inspired by these teachings to practice medicine. Church leaders—who taught that all illness was caused by God and could only be cured through worship—were worried by this development. They were particularly concerned about the practice of surgery (treatment involving operations and cutting open the body), which they saw as unsuitable work for a clergyman. So, in the twelfth century, the Church banned monks and priests from practicing surgery. As monks and priests were among the most educated people in Europe at this time, the ban held back progress in surgery. Unlike physicians, surgeons would not gain a professional status until well into the fourteenth century.

The Role of the Monasteries

One of the healthiest places to live in medieval Europe was a monastery. Monasteries were usually built in the middle of the countryside, where there was less danger of disease. Many monasteries had hospitals where patients were kept clean and given plenty of rest. Monks grew herbs and plants in their gardens, and often experimented with them to make medicines. They used these medicines, as well as the power of prayer, to treat their patients.

Church Hospitals

The Church's influence on medicine during this period was not wholly negative. Church leaders saw it as the duty of all Christians to help the less fortunate, and the Church established many hospitals to care for the sick. Abbeys and monasteries also had their own hospitals, some of which were open to members of the public. In all these hospitals the emphasis was on care rather than cure. Few of the staff had medical training, and they saw their role more as providing patients with rest and spiritual comfort rather than treatment.

Monks suffering from the plague are blessed by a priest in this fourteenth-century illustration. Prayer was often the only hope for people struck down by serious illnesses.

9

Medicine in the Middle Ages

DURING THE MIDDLE AGES, the medical community was composed of five divisions: physicians, surgeons, barber-surgeons, apothecaries, and unlicensed healers.

Physicians

In the eleventh century, people began to accept that formal medical education was necessary, and by the twelfth century medical schools were established in several European cities. Only those who graduated from these schools, known as physicians, were qualified to practice medicine. Physicians became the wealthiest and most important members of the medical community.

Physicians rarely touched their patients. Most were also members of the clergy, and considered it beneath them to make physical examinations. They were trained in the logical method of diagnosis. They would look at two opposing theories, for example

This fourteenth-century illustration shows twelve scenes in which a physician, wearing a traditional black cap and gown, is consulted about various illnesses. The physician needed only a description of the symptoms to make his diagnosis.

This poem by Enricus Cordus (1486–1535) expresses the feelings of many patients toward their physicians in the Middle Ages:

Three faces wears the doctor:
When first sought, An Angel's—
And a God's when the cure half wrought:
But when, that cure complete, he seeks his fee,
The Devil then looks less terrible than he.

Bartlett's Familiar Quotations

from Galen and Avicenna, and through debate reach a new theory. By using this method physicians could often make a diagnosis but they rarely cured their patients.

Surgeons

Surgeons stood second in the ranks of those who practiced medicine. Not many European medical schools offered courses in surgery and the majority of surgeons were not university educated. Surgeons did consult textbooks, but most of their knowledge was based on experience. They were seen as craftsmen, skilled at setting broken bones and closing wounds, as well as more complex forms of surgery (see page 12).

Barber-Surgeons

Barber-surgeons stood well below surgeons in the medical rankings. Most could not read and none went to a university. They usually worked as assistants to surgeons or physicians, carrying out less skillful tasks such as **cupping** (using a glass to increase blood supply to an area of skin) or applying a poultice (a warm moist preparation for easing pain). Barber-surgeons worked part-time and added to their income by shaving and cutting hair.

Apothecaries and Unlicensed Healers

Apothecaries were similar to present-day pharmacists. They prepared and sold herbs and spices as medical treatments. Apothecaries had no formal training and little understanding of the human body or the causes of disease.

Unlicensed healers were found mostly in rural areas. They had no formal training, yet it is likely they practiced all forms of medicine. Their low fees made them popular with the poor.

Medieval women often assisted during childbirth. These midwives were given no formal medical training, and they used skills that had been passed on from generation to generation.

The Role of Women

People who could not afford to see physicians often went to local women for treatment. Women were generally not allowed to practice medicine, and were barred from most medical schools. One woman, Jacoba Felicie, was tried in 1322 for practicing medicine without a license. She said in her defense: "Some women may be embarrassed by having to go to a man for a cure. I have proved my ability to cure and heal the sick. Surely it is better that I am allowed to make visits than patients die through the failures of a licensed doctor."

The Treatment of Illness and Disease

TREATMENTS for illness and disease during the Middle Ages were based on the theory of the four humors (see page 7). According to Galen and Avicenna, each humor was associated with a different element. Blood was hot and wet, like air; **phlegm** was cold and wet, like water; yellow **bile** was hot and dry, like fire; and black bile was cold and dry, like earth. The appeal of this theory—and perhaps one reason why it was not seriously challenged until the late fifteenth century—was that it made the human body seem like a tiny version of the world, containing the four elements: air, water, fire, and earth.

Restoring Balance

When the four humors were in balance, the body was in a healthy state, known as *eukrasia*. Imbalance of the humors led to sickness, or *dyskrasia*. Treatments were designed to restore the body to *eukrasia*. The first treatment suggested was rest, to allow the body to heal itself.

If this failed, the physician would try to work out which humor was out of balance, usually by observing the patient's external appearance and listening to their symptoms. Occasionally, the physician might analyze the patient's blood, feces, or urine, or take his or her pulse. This brief

A doctor selects some medicinal herbs in this fifteenth-century illustration. Plant-based remedies were often used to restore an imbalance of the humors.

12

Some medieval remedies:

To treat heartburn:

Take a crust of a white loaf that is right brown, and eat it when you go to bed; but do not drink thereafter, and so lie and sleep all night and that shall drive the heartburn away.

To treat loss of speech:

Take the juice of southern wood or of primrose, and he shall speak at once.

To make a man or woman sleep three days:

Take the gall of a hare, and give it in his food, and he shall not awake until his face is washed with vinegar.

English Historical Documents

examination was usually followed by a diagnosis and a prescription.

According to humor theory, most plants, foods, and other household items could be classed as either cold, hot, dry, or wet, and could therefore be used to modify the levels of humor within a person. For example, pasta (a warm food) could be used for "hot stomach," while linen (cold and dry) could be used to dry up oozing sores and ulcers.

Bloodletting and Herbal Remedies

If there was still no improvement in the patient, the physician might prescribe a surgical treatment such as bloodletting (see panel on page 12), **cautery** or cupping, or he might recommend an herbal remedy. Different herbs were associated with certain complaints. For example, a mixture of **henbane** and **hemlock** was used to cure painful thighs. Patients with stomach pain were told to chew laurel leaves, swallow the juice, and lay the leaves on their navel.

Bloodletting was performed on different parts of the body, depending on the condition. For example, melancholy (depression) might call for bleeding from a vein in the forehead.

Famine

BETWEEN the tenth and thirteenth centuries, Europe experienced steady population growth. This was partly due to a lack of infectious diseases, but there were other reasons, too. Innovations in agriculture and technology produced a food surplus in the tenth and eleventh centuries. Also, after two hundred years of almost constant warfare, eleventh- and twelfth-century Europe enjoyed a period of relative peace.

A Change in the Weather

This period of progress reached a peak in the first half of the thirteenth century. However, major climatic changes caused the weather to become colder and wetter after 1250, which was disastrous for agriculture. In these difficult times, farmers turned to their most productive crop: wheat.

Wheat produced higher yields than other crops, and so farmers turned all their fields over to wheat farming. In many areas animal farming was abandoned, causing a lack of protein in people's diets and a shortage of manure for fertilizer. This overreliance on wheat was a dangerous strategy—if the wheat crop failed, people would starve.

Despite a rapid fall in food productivity after 1250, Europe's population continued to increase. This was partly because men and women tended to marry young and have large families. This custom, which had begun during the period of prosperity, continued in spite of poor harvests.

This fifteenth-century illustration shows the different phases of the farming calendar. The cold, wet weather of the late thirteenth century made the soil waterlogged which killed off the seedlings.

Death in the Towns

The town populations of Europe suffered terribly in the years 1315–1322. Food stocks were exhausted, and the prices of many foods rose by over 500 percent. Towns like Ypres, Ghent, Bruges, and Louvain lost between 10 and 15 percent of their populations to famine. In 1320, similar numbers died in Italy and in England; many were reduced to eating dogs and cats.

14

This illustration shows famine victims lying dead. In Germany, during the 1316 famine, people were seen cutting down and eating the corpses of hanged criminals.

Farming in Crisis

In the late thirteenth and early fourteenth centuries, a growing population, combined with a colder climate and overreliance on wheat, led to a series of famines in Europe. The 1290s was a very rainy decade, and crops often rotted in the fields. In 1304 and 1305, northern France and the Netherlands suffered famine, and in 1309 Europe experienced its first continent-wide famine in over 250 years. A much worse general famine struck in 1316 when the wheat crop failed again. This had been set in motion by a wet spring in 1315 which made it impossible to plow all of the fields that were ready for cultivation. The spring and summer of 1316 were also cold and wet. Many peasant families were by now too weak from **malnutrition** to till the land needed for the harvest.

The following is taken from an account of the famine of 1315 in St. Albans, England:

"Hunger grew in the land.... Meat and eggs began to run out, capons and fowl could hardly be found, animals died of pest, swine could not be fed because of the excessive price of fodder.... The usual kinds of meat, suitable for eating, were too scarce; horse meat was precious; plump dogs were stolen. And, according to many reports, men and women in many places secretly ate their own children...."

Annates, Johannes de Trokelowe

Although the harvests had improved by 1318, a series of **epidemics** hit Europe's livestock populations between 1316 and 1325, sending farming into crisis once more.

Although they were devastating at the time, the famines of the early fourteenth century did not have a long-term impact on Europe's population. Fertility rates continued to rise, and the population had almost recovered to its 1300 level by the 1340s.

Death in Medieval Times

DEATH was a frequent visitor in the Middle Ages, and it came in many different forms. The poorest suffered the most. They were not given any support by the government, and had to rely on the charity of the Church, or richer citizens, to survive. In the colder months, many died for lack of food and shelter.

People were less able to resist disease in medieval times, because they knew far less than we do about diet and **nutrition**. They lacked vitamins due to a popular belief that fruit was not healthy, and the low levels of dairy products in people's diets led to weakened teeth and bones. Poorer people could only afford to eat meat on feast days, so they often suffered from insufficient protein.

In medieval art, death was often portrayed as a winged, skeletal figure with a large scythe, known as the Angel of Death.

The Dance of Death

Death was a popular subject in medieval art, perhaps because people's lives were so often cut short by war and disease. During the later Middle Ages, the Dance of Death began to appear in drama, poetry, music, and art. This was a procession or dance involving both living and dead people. The living—arranged in order of social rank, from the pope and emperor at the front, to beggars and hermits at the back—were led to their graves by the dead.

Food Storage

Sickness and death caused by eating bad food was a lot more common in medieval times. There was no way of keeping food refrigerated, except in winter, so most food had to be eaten fresh. Not all foods could be eaten at once, however, and much had to be stored. Grain, if badly stored, might become damp and infected by the ergot fungus (see page 5). Meat and fish were salted as a way of preserving them, and dogs were sometimes kept to test meat that had been around for a while. However, people were generally more willing to eat food that had gone a little bad, especially in times of shortages. Strong-flavored sauces were often used to disguise the unpleasant smell and taste of old meat.

Childbirth

Childbirth during the Middle Ages was very dangerous for both mother and infant. Records show that approximately 20 percent of women died during childbirth and 5 percent of babies died during delivery, with a further 10–12 percent dying in their first month. Women were generally assisted by midwives who lacked medical training and could do little if there were complications.

Living Conditions

Daily life could be very dangerous in the Middle Ages. In towns, open flames were used in houses for cooking and for light. Fires were also needed by bakers and blacksmiths for their work. Timber-framed buildings were built close together, and in such crowded conditions, it was all too easy for a fire, once lit, to burn out of control.

In farms, where most people lived, accidents were common. A person trampled by an animal, or injured by a sickle, was more likely to die than today. Without antiseptics, wounds frequently became infected. Also, transportation was slow and roads were poor, and there were often long delays before victims received medical attention.

Food was prepared over open fires in people's homes. A single spark could easily start a major fire.

Medieval Diseases: Leprosy

BETWEEN the tenth and thirteenth centuries, the disease that Europeans dreaded more than any other was leprosy, or Hansen's Disease. Leprosy **bacteria** multiply very slowly, and the disease is slow acting and not very infectious. It develops over a long period, giving its victims years of suffering. It is rarely fatal in itself, although it makes people vulnerable to other illnesses connected with the lungs or intestines.

A Disease of the Soul

Leprosy was feared because of its terrible effects on the appearance of its victims. The skin of lepers became scarred and blistered, and fingers, toes, and parts of the face would slowly rot away. The rotting parts would give off a terrible smell.

The Church believed that leprosy was a disease of the soul, caused by God and therefore incurable. It was believed to be the result of certain sins, especially lust and pride.

In some communities, lepers were required to ring a bell as they passed along the street to warn people of their presence.

Rules for Lepers

Many medieval towns created rules to guide lepers in their everyday lives. Lepers were banned from all shops, markets, churches, and other public places, and they were obliged to stand downwind from anyone who wished to speak to them. They had to wear special clothing to mark them out, and were not allowed to wash or drink at public water sources. Lepers were made to touch everything with a rod. Even public buildings could not be touched without gloves, and shoes had to be worn at all times.

With no means of supporting themselves, lepers relied on the goodwill of others, especially the Church, to survive.

Legally Dead

With no treatment available for lepers, the only solution was isolation. Once diagnosed, lepers were regarded as legally and spiritually dead. They had no rights, and a mass was sung for their soul. Earth was shoveled on the leper's feet to symbolize departure from life, and the patient was then sent to a leper hospital (also known as a lazar house) or colony to live out the rest of his or her days. For lepers, this would often mean separation from their husband or wife, and family. In some countries, a spouse was allowed to join the leper, although this was problematic as most leper colonies were exclusively male or female. Lazar houses were built in many European towns and cities between the eleventh and thirteenth centuries. Here lepers would live like monks, rising at different times of the night to pray to God.

Leprosy rose dramatically between the eighth and thirteenth centuries, then fell away, disappearing almost completely by 1400. Its sudden rise may have been due to the rise in Europe's population, which led to an increase in potential victims. Its fall is most likely explained by the plague (see pages 20–21) in the second half of the fourteenth century. Lepers, already weakened by their disease, were among the plague's first victims.

Gilbertus Anglicus (*c.* 1170–1230)

Gilbertus Anglicus was an English physician who came to prominence as the chancellor of the famous medical school at Montpellier (in France). He was skeptical of the Church's view that leprosy was incurable, and made a study of lepers over a number of years. Anglicus concluded that leprosy was not very contagious and was a disease that mostly affected the nerves. He believed it could be treated like other nerve-related diseases. However, his suggestions for a cure were ineffective, being based on balancing the body's humors—the popular theory of the time.

Medieval Diseases: Plague

BY FAR the worst disease of the Middle Ages—and perhaps the most devastating infection in human history—was plague. Plague does not come in isolated outbreaks, but in pandemics (a series of epidemics). There are three main forms of plague: bubonic, pneumonic, and septicemic.

Bubonic Plague

Bubonic plague, or the Black Death, is by far the most common form. It is transmitted to humans by the bite of a flea. The first sign that a person has caught it is the appearance of a small blackish area of inflamed skin around the bite. The lymph glands in the armpits, groin, or neck, become enlarged, and these painful swellings, known as **buboes**, can grow to the size of apples. Next the victim begins bleeding under the skin, causing red blotches to appear. Finally, the blotches turn black and the victim dies soon afterward.

The Hungry Flea

The flea responsible for spreading the plague was *Xenopsylla cheopis*, a bloodsucking parasite that lives on rodents and humans. The plague bacteria—***Yersina pestis***—grows inside the flea, blocking its stomach and causing it to become very hungry. The flea greedily bites its human host in an effort to satisfy its hunger. During the feeding process, the person's blood becomes infected with the plague bacteria, and the flea passes this blood back into the person's wound. The plague now has a new host.

The black rat was a carrier of the plague in European towns and cities. Black rats often made their nests in the roofs and dark corners of town houses. The fleas living on these rats then passed the plague on to humans.

A fourteenth-century engraving of a plague victim. Medieval people were not aware that farm animals, such as those shown here, could be plague carriers.

Pneumonic and Septicemic Plagues

Unlike other forms of plague, pneumonic plague can be transmitted from person to person. It can occur when there is a sharp drop in temperature and the infection moves to a victim's lungs. The victim feels very cold and coughs up a mixture of blood and phlegm. The coughed up mixture contains *Yersina pestis* and by this process it can be transmitted through the air to other people. Death occurs in 95 to 100 percent of cases. This makes it more lethal than bubonic plague, which kills 50 to 60 percent of its victims.

Septicemic plague is the rarest and deadliest form. Like bubonic, it is transmitted by fleabite, but in this case the bacteria enters the victim's bloodstream in massive numbers. A rash forms within hours, and death always occurs within a day, before buboes have time to form.

First Appearance

Plague first emerged in Europe in a pandemic that lasted from 541 to 762 A.D. The initial epidemic was known as Justinian's Plague after the **Byzantine** emperor of the time. Each epidemic would arrive between ten and twenty-four years after the last. It has been estimated that Europe lost between 50 and 60 percent of its population in the course of the pandemic.

Procopius, the Byzantine court historian, wrote about the symptoms of Justinian's Plague in the 540s:

"They [the infected person] had a sudden fever, some when just roused from sleep.... [In] the particular part of the body which is called the groin, that is, below the abdomen, but also inside the armpits, and in some cases besides the ears, and at different points on the thighs came a large swelling or bubo."

History of the Wars, Procopius

The Causes of the Black Death

SOME TIME in the late thirteenth or early fourteenth century, bubonic plague spread outward from the Gobi Desert in Mongolia—a permanent location of *Yersina pestis*. It spread east to China, south to India, and west toward the Middle East and the Mediterranean.

How the Plague Spread

Two theories have been put forward to explain this spread. First, the plague bacteria may have infected the rodents that traveled with the supply trains of **Mongol** horsemen in the Gobi Desert. The Mongols were a **nomadic** people who dominated large parts of Asia, Persia, and China at that time. Their horsemen provided a system of communications across their vast empire, and they may have helped to spread the plague east, south, and west.

A second theory suggests that in the late thirteenth and early fourteenth centuries, parts of Asia became hotter and drier. This caused farmers and wild animals from central Asia to move westward in search of food and water. As they moved west, Asian rodents may have infected local rats with the plague.

A Mongol archer on horseback. The Mongols seemed to understand the connection between certain rodents and the plague. They forbade the trapping of some animals and refused to wear their furs.

The Tatar Siege of Caffa

Some people claimed that the Black Death entered Europe following the 1345 siege by the Tatars of the Genoese city of Caffa in the Crimea (in present-day Ukraine). Plague broke out in the Tatar army during the siege, and they resorted to catapulting their dead over the city walls. The rotting bodies were said to spread the plague and soon the Genoese were fleeing back to Italy, taking the Black Death with them as they crossed Europe. This account seems doubtful because the plague needs a living host to spread. It cannot pass itself on from corpses. It is more likely, if anything, that wild rodents infected Caffa's population.

The map legend reads:

The Spread of the Black Death
- 1347
- 1348
- 1349
- 1350
- 1351
- unaffected areas
- ● towns badly affected by plague
- ○ towns not badly affected by plague

This map shows how the Black Death spread over a period of four years from western Asia to North Africa and southern Europe, and finally to northern Europe.

Whatever the cause, by the early 1330s the plague had struck parts of China. Between 1330 and 1346, the westward spread of the plague was helped by the east-west trading system, including overland and sea routes, that linked China and India with Europe. The overland route that carried goods by **caravan** from northern China through central and western Asia was probably most responsible for the plague's spread. However, ships were also known to carry infected Asian rats.

The Plague Arrives

The plague arrived in Europe in October 1347, when some Genoese merchant ships returned to Sicily from the Black Sea. When the ships docked at Syracuse, many on board were already dying of the plague. Within days the disease had spread to the city and the surrounding countryside. Soon it reached the great cities of Italy, such as Genoa, Florence, Rome, and Venice, where death rates reached 40 or even 50 percent of the population.

The Black Death

BY JANUARY 1348, the disease had spread beyond Italy and reached Marseilles in France. By late spring it was in Paris, the largest city in northern Europe. During the hot summer months the city's death toll rose, reaching a peak in late autumn when it was reported that eight hundred people died each day. In total around a third of Paris's population was wiped out by the Black Death.

The Plague Reaches Northern Europe

In September 1348, the Black Death arrived in England, and by the end of that year, it had spread to Scotland, Norway, and Germany. Between June and September 1349, London suffered an average of 290 deaths per day. By the spring of 1350, between 35 and 40 percent of London's population had been killed. Even worse hit was East Anglia where in just five months in 1349, a third of the population died.

In the great majority of cases, the Black Death took the form of bubonic plague, spreading to humans after infecting

Greenland

Perhaps the most devastating visitation of the Black Death occurred in Greenland. By the tenth century, this cold country to the far northwest of Europe had been settled by Norwegians and Icelanders. These settlements were sometimes visited by supply ships from Scandinavia, and this is probably how the plague spread there in the winter of 1350. In the late twelfth century there were around six thousand to seven thousand Norse living in three settlements in Greenland. But after the plague's arrival, its Scandinavian settlements appear to have been wiped out altogether.

Plague victims are buried at Tournai, an important textile town on the border of France and the Netherlands. The plague reached here in 1349.

local rat populations. Occasionally it would take on its pneumonic, or even its septicemic forms. Scandinavia, like East Anglia and Italy, suffered very high death tolls—in some areas up to 50 percent of the population died.

In the winter of 1348, the plague seemed to disappear, but this was only because fleas are **dormant** in the cold months. The Black Death struck again the following spring, and for the next four years it continued to kill new victims. By 1352, around 25 million people had died—one third of Europe's population.

Victims of the Plague

The plague spared no one: princes and peasants were equally at risk. In Avignon, France, one third of the cardinals died while England lost three archbishops in the space of eighteen months. Even King Alfonso XI of Castile (in present-day Spain) died.

Throughout Europe, bodies piled up in the streets as people died faster than they could be buried. Many corpses were thrown into mass graves, including two thousand in a single site in London. At sea, ghost ships were encountered, whose entire crews had been wiped out.

John of Fordun, a late-fourteenth-century priest of Aberdeen Cathedral, wrote a chronicle of Scottish history. He witnessed the Black Death in Scotland, and left this account:

"In the year 1350 there was in the kingdom of Scotland so great a pestilence and plague among men ... as, from the beginning of the world even unto modern times, had never been heard of by men.... For to such a pitch did the plague wreak its cruel spite that nearly a third of mankind were thereby made to pay the debt of nature. Moreover, by God's will, this evil led to a strange and unwonted [unexpected] kind of death, insomuch that the flesh of the sick was sometimes puffed out and swollen, and they dragged out their earthly life for barely two days."

Chronicle, John Fordun

Explanations for the Black Death

THE BLACK DEATH brought panic to Europe. Churches stopped holding masses, peasants stopped plowing their fields, merchants closed their shops, and taxes went uncollected. Even the long-running war between England and France was suspended in 1349, only to be resumed in 1355.

Various explanations were given for the plague, ranging from lust with old women to overeating. Many, including church leaders, believed it to be a punishment from God. Others blamed certain groups of people such as women or lepers, who were suspected of practicing witchcraft or poisoning the water. Medical authorities were divided. Some claimed it was caused by a corruption of the air due to a particular **conjunction** of the planets (see panel); others believed it came from poisonous fumes from the earth's core, released to the surface by earthquakes.

Flagellants

The most popular theory, however, was that plague was God's punishment for the sins of the world. Among those who held this opinion were the Flagellants. These were religious people who wandered in bands through the towns and villages of Europe, beating themselves with leather whips and singing hymns to atone for the

In medieval times, astrologers were often consulted about matters of health. In this fourteenth-century illustration, a king is advised by a physician (left) and an astrologer.

Blaming the Planets

In 1348, a group of physicians at the University of Paris made an in-depth study of the plague. They concluded that it had been caused by an unfortunate conjunction of Saturn, Jupiter, and Mars which had occurred at 1 o'clock in the afternoon on March 20, 1345, and had caused the earth to exhale poisonous vapors. The physicians recommended avoiding fatty meat, fish, and sleeping during the daytime.

A line of Flagellants in the Netherlands in 1349. In October 1349, Pope Clement VI issued a bull (papal order) condemning the practice, and by 1350 the movement had almost completely disappeared.

evil of their fellow humans. The Flagellants traveled two by two in long columns of up to three hundred. They did not bathe, shave, or change their clothing, and could not speak without the permission of their master. At each town, they would gather outside the church. The men would then remove their shirts and whip themselves as they walked in a circle.

Attacks on the Jews

Many blamed the plague on the Jews, who were often the targets of persecution during the Middle Ages. News of the spreading plague prompted **pogroms** in many European towns, including Brussels (in present-day Belgium), and Stuttgart, Lindau, Ulm, Dresden, and Speyer (all in present-day Germany). Although some towns protected their Jewish residents, several such as Zurich (in present-day Switzerland), expelled them.

Pope Clement VI pointed out that the Jews were suffering from the plague just as much as Christians, and he issued two bulls (papal orders) in 1348 forbidding the slaughter of Jews. Despite this, hundreds of Jews were burned to death in the towns of Basle (in present-day Switzerland), and Strasbourg, Frankfurt-am-Main, Mainz, and Cologne (all in present-day Germany).

Jean de Froissart, a contemporary writer, describes the Flagellants:

"The penitents went about, coming first out of Germany. They were men who did public penance and scourged [whipped] themselves with whips of hard knotted leather with little iron spikes. Some made themselves bleed very badly between the shoulder blades and some foolish women had cloths ready to catch the blood and smear it on their eyes, saying it was miraculous blood."

Chronicles, Jean de Froissart

27

Treatments for the Plague

FEW SUSPECTED that the common rat, an everyday sight on medieval city streets, was to blame for the Black Death. However, physicians recognized that people close to, or in contact with, plague victims were likely to be infected, and they recommended that people flee from infected areas.

When the plague struck, some doctors took their own advice and fled, but others stayed behind to do their duty to their patients. They would try bloodletting and cupping in an area close to the buboes, since they believed that this was where the body was being attacked. These methods were completely ineffective, and in many cases caused death.

A recipe for Edward IV's plague medicine:

"Take five cups of rue [a plant with bitter tasting leaves], five crops of tansy [a plant of the daisy family], five little blades of columbine [a plant with blue flowers], and a great quantity of marigold flowers. Then take a newly laid egg and make a hole in either end, and blow out all that's inside it. Lay it next to the fire and let it roast until it can be ground to powder. Then add the ground eggshell and crushed herbs to a quantity of treacle and mix this with good ale and make the sick person drink it for three evenings and three mornings. If the patient holds it down, he will survive."

The Black Death, Robert S. Gottfried

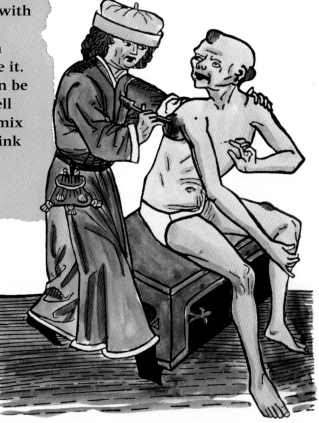

Islamic doctors recommended lancing the buboes and then applying an ointment made from Armenian Clay, a substance praised by Galen for its healing properties.

A Deadly Vapor

Most people believed that the plague was transmitted on the air, and they burned incense to ward off the deadly vapor. Popular scents included juniper, pine, laurel, beech, lemon leaves, rosemary, and camphor. When venturing out of their houses, people covered their faces with handkerchiefs dipped in aromatic oils.

Numerous remedies, charms, and spells were prescribed by wise old women and apothecaries. Drinking elderberry juice every day or wearing a jade necklace was supposed to give protection from the plague. There was no science behind these treatments, but desperate people were willing to try anything.

Dishes of fresh milk were left on the lips of victims to absorb the plague poison; herds of oxen and cows were driven through the streets in the hope that their good, clean breath would neutralize the bad city air; goats were kept in bedrooms in the belief that the bad air in a house could be driven out by a powerful smell.

Isolation

The only effective action against the Black Death seems to have been taken by city authorities. In Italy the authorities realized that the way to contain the plague was to isolate the people with the disease from the rest of the population. In Milan, houses inhabited by plague victims were immediately walled up, isolating both the healthy and the sick within them. The authorities in Venice forbade any incoming ships from docking in their harbor. Cities that took measures such as these tended to suffer fewer casualties.

Some physicians realized there was no cure for plague. They simply advised victims to get plenty of rest, drink lots of fluid, and apply herbal ointments to their buboes.

Because plague was thought to be incurable, many of the writings from the time focused on how to prevent catching it in the first place. This contemporary poem, "Dietary and Doctrine for the Pestilence," by English monk, John Lydgate, is one example:

**"Who will be whole and keep him from sickness
And resist the stroke of pestilence
Let him be glad and void of all heaviness
Flee wicked aire, eschew [avoid] the violence
Drink good wine and wholesome meats take
Walk in clean aire, eschew mists black."**

Lydgate's Minor Poems, II, John Lydgate

The Plague Returns

THE BLACK DEATH lasted until the end of 1351. By 1360, the population of Europe was beginning to rise again but in 1361, the second epidemic of the pandemic—known as *Pestis secunda*— broke out in Europe.

Return of the Nightmare

To the people of medieval Europe, who were starting to put the experience of the Black Death behind them, it was like the return of a nightmare. While not as deadly as the Black Death, *Pestis secunda* was still one of the most devastating epidemics in human history, killing between 10 and 20 percent of the population, especially children born after the Black Death, and members of the **nobility**. In England, for example, the upper classes lost about a quarter of their number.

One of the last appearances of the plague was in Marseilles, France, in 1720. A ship from Syria landed at the port with several plague victims on board. By 1722 more than half of Marseilles's population had died. In this painting the dead bodies are being piled into a cart and being taken away for burial.

Plague Doctors

In several European countries, physicians and surgeons were hired by city authorities to treat plague victims. It was a highly dangerous and unpleasant job, and when it was finished, the plague doctor was isolated for a long period for reasons of safety. Not surprisingly, few established physicians were interested in doing this job. It was usually done by young doctors, often from rural areas, still hoping to make their mark.

In 1471, England was engulfed in another plague epidemic. John Paston, a Norfolk gentleman living in London, wrote home to his family:

"I pray you send me word if any of our friends or well-wishers be dead, for I fear that there is a great death in Norwich ... for I assure you that this is the most universal death that I ever witnessed in England. For, by my troth, I can hear from pilgrims who travel through the country that no man who rides or goes in any country or borough town in England is free from the sickness."

The Paston Letters

Pestis secunda lasted until spring 1362. A third epidemic occurred in 1369, killing a further 10 to 15 percent of Europe's population, and convincing the people of the time that it had become a regular part of their lives. Outbreaks of the disease continued to occur every five to twelve years for the next 350 years, and did not disappear completely until the late eighteenth century. As a result, it was not until the mid–sixteenth century that Europe regained its population levels of the thirteenth century.

Other Diseases

Plague was not the only disease that people were confronted with in this period. During the fourteenth and fifteenth centuries, European children also fell victim to smallpox, or the red plague as it was sometimes called. In northern France during the 1440s, more people died from smallpox than from bubonic plague.

Worse still were diseases of the bowel, caused by poor sanitation and the presence of sewage in water sources. Most at risk were children, and diarrhea was a major cause of death among the young. **Dysentery** frequently swept through armies, often killing more soldiers than were felled on the battlefield. In 1473, an epidemic of dysentery wiped out 15 to 20 percent of the adult male population of East Anglia in just three months.

A doctor treats a smallpox victim. Survivors of smallpox became immune to the disease, but it could be deadly to those who had never had it, especially children.

Consequences of the Plague

THE IMMEDIATE REACTION to the Black Death was shock, and in many areas life came to a complete standstill. Some people took advantage of the breakdown of society, and indulged in whatever pleasures took their fancy. Others went the opposite way and became more religious. Many gave to charity or went on pilgrimages in the hope of **salvation**.

The Church

The Church itself mostly failed in its duty to provide spiritual comfort. Many parish priests fled, leaving no one to comfort the sick or deliver last rites. There were exceptions, however, and the high death rate among **friars** does suggest that many of them remained to look after victims.

The Church was also damaged by its association with the medical profession. Most physicians were also members of the clergy, and when they failed to provide advice or treatment for the sick, it made the Church seem powerless at a time of crisis.

A Fascination with Death

With so many people dying from the plague, there was a growing obsession with the rituals of death. Funerals often turned into celebrations, and gravestones became more elaborate. Those

A priest reads from the Bible before a body is buried.

The Italian writer, Giovanni Boccaccio, describes how some people reacted to the plague:

"Others ... held that plenty of drinking and enjoyment, singing and free living and the gratification of the appetite in every possible way, letting the devil take the hindmost, was the best preventative of such a malady...."

The Decameron, Giovanni Boccaccio

In this fifteenth-century illustration, Death does not discriminate based on status: it takes a priest, a laborer, a friar, and a child.

who could afford them built monuments to their loved ones, and made **death masks** of their faces.

The art and literature of the time reflected this new fascination. The painter, Francesco Triani, showed death as a hideous old woman in a black cloak with snakelike hair, bulging eyes, clawed feet, and a scythe to collect her victims. The post-plague writings of Boccaccio (see box on page 32) were often about death.

Social Change

The Black Death brought about major changes to the social order. The fact that there were fewer people around caused a labor shortage and a food surplus. This was good news for the surviving **peasantry** who were now able to move from place to place, and demand better wages and conditions.

For the nobility it was a disaster, and many noble families died out for lack of a male heir. Another social consequence of the plague was a general breakdown in law and order, and a rise in rebelliousness among the peasantry (see panel).

The English Peasants' Revolt

In England the peasantry wanted to preserve the greater freedom of movement and higher wages brought about by the plague. When, in 1381, they were faced with a series of new taxes, they rebelled. The Peasants' Revolt was led by a wealthy peasant named Wat Tyler and a priest called John Ball. The rebels regarded the nobles and the clergy as their enemy. They beheaded the Archbishop of Canterbury, and looted and burned parts of London. In the end, the nobility restored order and the rebels were punished. Nevertheless, the revolt was a success because the new taxes were abolished.

The Birth of Modern Medicine

THE MEDICAL COMMUNITY had failed to find any answer to the Black Death. Its knowledge was based on texts hundreds of years old which were useless in the face of the new disease. The rigid structure of the profession, which kept physicians and surgeons apart from each other, meant that physicians had little understanding of human anatomy and most surgeons had no understanding of medical theory.

Over the previous two hundred years, medicine had become more professional with the establishment of medical schools, and more qualified physicians and surgeons. However, progress was slow, and it was the plague—followed by *Pestis secunda*—that brought about the birth of modern medicine.

The Rise of Surgery

One important change was the rise in status of surgeons (see pages 38–39). With the failure of theory-based medicine, many doctors turned their attention to the practical craft of surgery. Universities began offering courses in anatomy and surgery. Human corpses were cut up for study (despite the objections of the Church), books on anatomy were published, and surgeons began to take their place alongside physicians at the top of the profession.

Public Health and Sanitation

Attitudes toward public health and cleanliness in towns and cities became more modern in the wake of the plague (see pages 42–43). People were aware that dirty conditions could lead to disease. Boards of health were established

Thomas Linacre (c. 1460–1524)

One of the people most responsible for improving standards in English medicine in the fifteenth and early sixteenth centuries was Thomas Linacre. Linacre went overseas to train, studying medicine at Padua in Italy where he later became Professor of Anatomy. He returned to England and became one of Henry VIII's physicians. Linacre translated several medical works from Greek into Latin, and in 1518 he established the Royal College of Physicians. For a physician to work in London, he first had to gain a license from the college. This process helped to raise standards in medicine.

This illustration of a corpse being dissected is from a 1345 book on surgery by Guy of Pavia, one of the earliest books of its kind.

in several Italian cities. In the German city of Nuremberg, streets were paved and regularly cleaned. Rubbish could not be dumped in the street, but had to be bagged and carted away.

Hospitals

The word *hospital* comes from the Latin *hospes*, which means guest, stranger, or foreigner. The original purpose of hospitals was to provide shelter for travelers of all kinds. Later they began to cater to the poor, the old, and the sick. Usually they were run by monks or nuns with little or no medical training. No cures were available, but patients were generally served with fresh food, and the monks and nuns prayed for their souls. Following the Black Death, hospitals started to become more like the institutions we know of today (see pages 40–41).

Physicians analyze a urine sample and check the pulse of their patients in this fifteenth-century illustration. Although more hospitals were being founded, soldiers were still treated in tents near the battlefields where they fell.

The Printing Press

When Johannes Gutenberg developed the first printing press in the 1440s, he played an important part in revolutionizing European medicine. Before this time, books had to be copied out by hand, making it much harder for physicians and surgeons to share their knowledge and discoveries. With the invention of printing, books became cheaper and far more plentiful. Printed literature spread across Europe in a variety of languages, speeding up the learning process for medical students, and helping to improve the quality and quantity of medical care available.

Medical Schools

BY THE TIME of the Black Death, Europe had six leading medical schools. These were based in Salerno, Bologna, and Padua in Italy, Montpellier and Paris in France, and Oxford in England.

Salerno

The first medical school in Europe since ancient times was established in the ninth century at Salerno in Italy. Salerno was a port city, where travelers from throughout the Mediterranean world would gather, including educated Arabs with knowledge of the ancient Greek medical theories. The school began as a very informal institution with no set plan for training, just discussion groups between experts and students. By the late eleventh century the Salerno school was famous throughout Europe.

This fourteenth-century translation of Galen's works shows Galen teaching his students. His theories dominated medical schools until the fifteenth century.

Montpellier

By the thirteenth century Salerno was no longer the great school it had been, and Montpellier—established in the twelfth century—had become the leading medical school in Europe. Montpellier benefited from very strict entry requirements and its association with leading Jewish physicians (who were banned from other schools) from Spain and North Africa. Montpellier-trained doctors, such as Henri de Mondeville (*c.* 1260–1320) and Guy de Chauliac (see page 39), were famous throughout Europe.

The staff at the Salerno medical school published a poem near the beginning of the twelfth century. It was dedicated to the King of England and gave some practical advice on matters of health. Here is part of it:

**"With water cold to wash your hands and eyes,
In gentle fashion retching [emptying] every member [orifice],
And to refresh your braine when as you rise,
In heat, in cold, in July and December,
Both comb your head, and rub your teeth likewise."**

The Englishman's Doctor, **Or,** *The School of Salerne*

Bologna and Paris

Bologna became famous in the thirteenth century for pioneering the subject of surgery, which most other schools refused even to teach. The **dissection** of human corpses began there in the 1260s (see panel).

By the 1340s, Paris was generally considered to have the leading European medical school. It was certainly the richest, thanks to the financial support of the French royalty and the Church. It may not have been as original and pioneering as Bologna, but it could afford to attract the most famous teachers.

After the Plague

Following the Black Death, European medical schools began to recognize the limitations of trying to treat modern diseases on the basis of thousand-year-old theories. The northern European schools began to recruit surgeons, as Italian universities had done since the twelfth century. Anatomy and surgery became important parts of the medical curriculum at Paris, and these subjects were expanded at Bologna and Padua.

Cutting up corpses remained a problem in the days before refrigeration. At Bologna, dissections had previously only taken place in winter months and in the course of one day. After the plague, despite the problems of **decomposition**, dissections took place throughout the year and were done much more slowly. As a result, more was learned, and anatomy books became more accurate.

An illustration from Guy de Chauliac's famous book, **Surgery** *(1363), shows students observing the dissection of a body. It differed from previous medical works, being based on practical experience rather than theory.*

William of Saliceto (c. 1210–1277)

William of Saliceto, the leading professor at the Bologna medical school, was probably one of the earliest surgeons to dissect human corpses. Saliceto pioneered new techniques in surgery, such as the use of the knife instead of cautery. He taught that pus in a wound was a bad thing, and he was the first to join severed nerves together. He also tried to improve the status of surgeons and bring the disciplines of surgery and medicine closer together. Saliceto is most famous for his book *Surgery* [*Chirurgia*], published in 1275, which contains the earliest record of a human dissection.

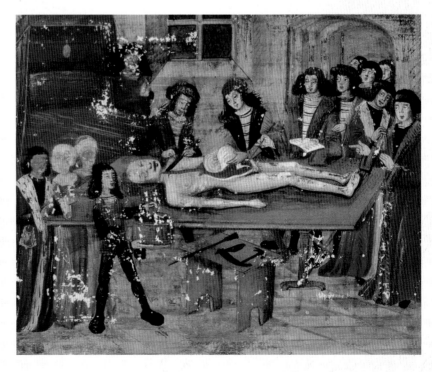

Surgery and Surgeons

IN THE YEARS following the Black Death, surgery became a respectable profession. Surgeons completely separated themselves from the more lowly barber-surgeons, and based more of their training on books and study, rather than on-the-job experience. The books they read, however, were not the ancient texts referred to by the physicians, but modern instruction manuals written by practicing surgeons.

From as early as 1348, surgeons began taking their place alongside physicians as doctors in many European cities. They were allowed to do **postmortems** on plague victims in Florence, Montpellier, and many other cities.

The rise of surgery was remarkably rapid. For example, in 1348, the rulers of Venice fined the surgeon Andreas of Padua for acting like a physician, though he had cured more than a hundred plague sufferers. However, only a year later, they named another surgeon, Nicholas of Ferrara, one of their finest doctors.

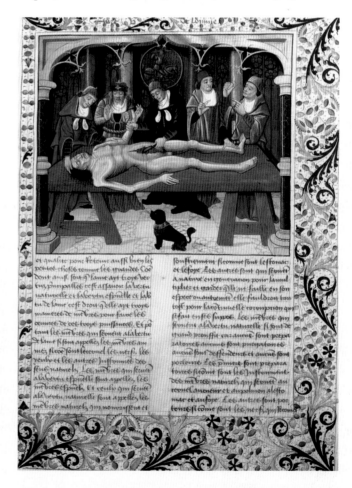

An illustration from **Book of the Properties of Things**, *written in the fifteenth century by Barthelemy l'Anglais. This book, written in French, was one of a growing number of modern-language texts.*

Henri de Mondeville in his book *Surgery* has this to say about bedside manner:

"[The surgeon] may temper and soften his warnings, or keep silent altogether if the patient is faint hearted or good natured…. The surgeon should also promise that if the patient can endure his illness and will obey … he will soon be cured and will escape all of the dangers which have been pointed out to him; thus the cure can be brought about more easily and quickly."

Surgery, Henri de Mondeville

An illustration of a surgeon's clinic, from **Surgery.** *Surgical books from this time often included descriptions of actual operations.*

Joining the Elite

In 1348, surgeons from Oxford were allowed to form a guild (an association of craftspeople) separate from and with authority over the barber-surgeons, and they were soon able to lecture at the university's medical school. Between 1352 and 1362, boards of surgeons were established in London to control surgical practice in the city.

By the end of the fourteenth century, surgeons were recognized throughout Europe as members of the medical elite. They were educated and university qualified, and were also seen as men of practical ability who achieved results where physicians failed.

Modern Language Texts

The surgeons' rise in status was helped by the growing number of medical books written in modern European languages. Until the 1340s, almost all medical books were written in Latin, which was then the accepted language of university-educated people throughout Europe. Surgeons, who lacked the university background of physicians at this time, preferred to communicate in their native language.

This demand for modern language texts continued even when surgeons began entering the university in the 1440s. This was because Latin as a spoken and written language was in decline, partly due to the number of Latin scholars that had died in the Black Death. By 1400, most medical textbooks were written in modern European languages.

Guy de Chauliac (c. 1300–1368)

One of the most famous doctors of the late fourteenth century was the surgeon Guy de Chauliac. He studied medicine at the universities of Montpellier, Paris, and Bologna, and practiced in the French cities of Montpellier, Lyons, and Avignon. He was surgeon to the King of France and to three popes. His great work, *Surgery*, was one of the most popular medical books of the time. It contained detailed descriptions of surgical treatments and remained a reference work for medical students until the eighteenth century.

Hospitals

THE BLACK DEATH and *Pestis secunda* prompted great changes to the medical profession and hospitals in the late fourteenth century. Traditionally, hospitals had been places built to isolate the sick, rather than to cure them. Hospitals were not particularly clean, and they offered little in the way of treatment for their patients. Some even took on widows, orphans, and paying guests. In the 1350s, many hospitals began for the first time to try to cure their patients. Their methods were basic, and few people were made better, but the purpose of hospitals had changed.

Hospital Wards

In order to achieve this new goal of curing people, hospitals had to become more professional and better organized. Most were divided into wards, each dealing with a different kind of ailment, such as broken bones or infectious diseases. Each ward contained between fifty and a hundred beds

Monks and doctors treat the sick in this wall painting from a fifteenth-century hospital in Siena, Italy. The presence of animals indicates that hospitals were still not very hygienic.

The rules of the Hospital of St. John in Bridgewater, Somerset, England were laid down in 1219 by Bishop Joscelin of Bath and Wells. They included the following pronouncements:

"No lepers, lunatics, or persons having the falling sickness or other contagious disease, and no pregnant women, or suckling infants, and no intolerable persons, even though they be poor and infirm, may be admitted to this house, and if any be admitted by mistake, they are to be expelled as soon as possible. And when the other poor and infirm persons have recovered, they are to be put out without delay."

The Register of Thomas Bekynton, Bishop of Bath and Wells 1443–1465

arranged in two rows along each side of the room, with an aisle down the center, just like in modern hospitals. This gave the staff easier access for treatment and cleaning.

The beds were placed under the windows, providing light and air in the summer, but often making them cold and drafty in the winter. Patients frequently had to share their beds with strangers, but the sheets were regularly cleaned. Most hospitals also benefited from running water and drains to carry away the waste.

Hospitals and Medicine

To help them achieve their new goal of curing people, hospitals began forming closer links with the world of medicine. Some farsighted hospitals had already made such connections. For example, students at Montpellier had done part of their training at a local hospital since the 1250s. For most hospitals, such reforms would not occur for another hundred years.

In the postplague era, many hospitals began developing libraries of medical books and arranged visits by local doctors. Medical students at Cambridge University gained firsthand experience by assisting with patients in a hospital in nearby Bury St. Edmunds. By the late fifteenth century, many hospitals were employing doctors full-time. The hospital of Santa Maria Nuova in Florence had nine doctors on its staff in 1500.

Hôtel Dieu

The Hôtel Dieu was a large hospital in Paris. Following the plague, it made major reforms to its organization and approach. Standards of cleanliness rose: walls were washed with lime twice a year, and bedding was cleaned weekly by a laundry staff of fifteen women. This was certainly necessary because in busy periods there might be three or four patients to a bed. On entering the hospital, patients were also given gowns to wear. Fresh food was served, including meat four or five times a week. Each ward had several bathtubs, and patients' hair was washed and cut regularly.

Nuns care for their patients at the Hôtel Dieu in Paris. With up to two hundred patients, the hospital was expensive to run, and patients who could afford it were expected to make a donation.

Public Health and Sanitation

BEFORE THE PLAGUE, public health in European cities was generally in a very poor state. Garbage was left to rot in the streets, human waste was thrown out of windows or dumped in local streams. City authorities did not think it was their responsibility to provide facilities for the disposal of waste, and they found it difficult to enforce laws preventing the public from dumping trash where they pleased.

Boards of Health

All this changed after the Black Death. Although no one knew exactly what caused the disease, they suspected that it spread more easily in the dirty environments of towns and cities. Throughout Europe, public health laws were passed, and boards of health were established in many cities. This process began in Venice, Florence, and Milan in Italy and then spread to other European cities.

In the fourteenth and fifteenth centuries, many towns and cities had communal bathhouses, offering steam baths and water baths. These were not intended to clean the body's surface, but to cause people to sweat, ridding themselves of harmful humors.

A member of the Milanese board of health reported an attack by local citizens:

"[We] were execrated [hated] by the ignorant populace [citizens], which listened to a few physicians, who, caring little for the public health, kept saying that there was no question of plague ... the populace began to slander and when by accident [we] moved through narrow streets of the popular quarters [we] were even pelted with stones."

Public Health and the Medical Profession in the Renaissance, by Carlo Cipolla

At first these boards were concerned only with preventing the spread of plague, and they were dissolved when the outbreak was over. However, when the plague kept returning, the boards became permanent institutions. The health board of Venice, which was typical of Italian cities, was structured as follows: Three noblemen were appointed Commissioners of the Public Health. They appointed full-time health officials to watch over each district of Venice.

The function of the public health boards was first to report an epidemic to the city authorities, and then to try to prevent it from spreading, usually by quarantine (enforced isolation). This rarely worked, as the quarantines were concerned only with isolating people—no one suspected that the city rats and their fleas were the real transmitters of the plague. Infected areas of the city were sealed off, and movement into or out of these areas was only permitted on presentation of a special pass issued by the board, confirming the person's good health.

Unpopular

By the late fifteenth century, the boards had become very powerful. They had more powers to enforce the proper dumping of garbage and sewage. They also had responsibilities for checking the quality of foods and drugs for sale and the cleanliness of hospitals and inns. Many townspeople came to resent the health boards for the restrictions they placed on their daily activities, and there were many cases of verbal abuse and even violence toward health officials.

Quarantine

During the time of the Black Death, it became clear to the Venetian authorities that many of the ships returning from the eastern Mediterranean were infected with the plague. The authorities ruled that ships were to be isolated for a certain period to give time for the plague to appear and then run its course. The period of isolation was set at forty days, and known as the *quarantina* (*quaranta* is forty in Italian) from which we get the word *quarantine*. In 1423, Venice set up its first quarantine station on an island near the city. Their system became the basis for quarantine control in cities throughout Europe.

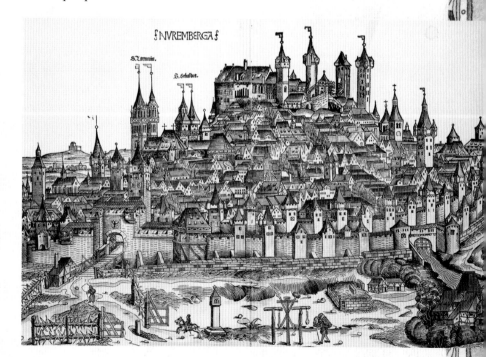

The city of Nuremberg, an important trading center in medieval times, had unusually high standards of public health. It boasted fourteen public baths, and the city's health board employed six full-time physicians and many more surgeons, apothecaries, and midwives.

The Dawn of a New Era

IN THE LATE FIFTEENTH CENTURY, disease patterns changed in Europe. Old diseases changed their nature, and new diseases appeared. After 1480, the period between outbreaks of plague became much longer, averaging every twenty years, allowing population levels to recover. Influenza, another common infectious disease of the period, began appearing in new forms, such as sweating sickness, which broke out in northwestern Europe in 1485, killing up to 10 percent of the population in some areas.

New diseases that appeared at this time included typhus, also known as jail fever, caused by dirty living conditions and bad diet. Syphilis—the most deadly of sexually transmitted diseases—also arrived in Europe for the first time in the 1490s.

With Columbus's discovery of the Americas in 1492, European diseases were carried to the New World, especially smallpox, measles, and **diphtheria**. Smallpox in particular devastated the population of Mexico, which fell to one-tenth of its previous level within fifty years of the arrival of the Europeans.

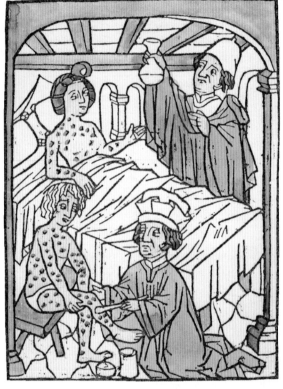

Doctors treat patients suffering from syphilis. In 1493, the disease spread so rapidly through the army of the French king Charles VIII that he had to abandon his 1493 siege of Naples.

The Spread of Syphilis

There are two theories to explain the arrival of syphilis in Europe in the late fifteenth century. At the time, many believed that the crews of Columbus's ships brought it back with them on their return from the Americas. The disease was well-established among the natives of Central America, and Columbus's return certainly coincided with a steep rise in the disease. However, according to the second theory, African slaves, brought to Europe by the Portuguese, suffered from a skin disease called yaws. In the cooler European climate, this turned into syphilis.

Changing Attitudes

Between 1000 and 1500, European attitudes toward health and disease changed a great deal. In that time, Europe's population had been largely reduced by the Black Death and further plague epidemics. This led to reforms in the medical community.

By 1500, physicians had become more professional. They were beginning to analyze symptoms rather than relying on ancient theories, and they understood a little more about the importance of diet, rest, and personal cleanliness. Surgeons could perform quite complex operations and hospitals were offering treatment by staff with medical knowledge. The public health boards had also begun the process of cleaning up cities.

Despite these advances, doctors were still ignorant of many things in 1500. Humor theory (see panel on page 7) remained the major principle behind most medical treatments, and cupping, cauterizing, and bloodletting were still widespread practices. It was only in 1616 that it was discovered that blood circulated around the body, while the true cause of plague was not learned until 1898.

However, the reforms of the medieval period laid the groundwork for the major achievements in science and medicine during the centuries that followed.

Many of those in Henry VIII of England's court fell sick with the sweating sickness. The king feared catching the disease himself. The French ambassador to the English court wrote in 1528:

"One of the *filles de chambre* of Mlle Boleyn was attacked on Tuesday by the sweating sickness. The King left in great haste, and went a dozen miles off.... This disease is the easiest in the world to die of. You have a slight pain in the head and at the heart; all at once you begin to sweat.... It is true that if you merely put your hand out of bed during the first twenty-four hours ... you become stiff as a poker."

The Illustrated Treasury of Medical Curiosa, Art Newman

The use of leeches to draw out infected blood, as shown in this fifteenth-century illustration, was continued by some doctors until well into the twentieth century.

Chronology

c. 400 B.C.	Theory of the four humors is developed, probably by Hippocrates.
165 A.D.	Smallpox first emerges in Europe.
c. 200	Galen makes the first in-depth study of anatomy.
251	Measles first emerges in Europe.
541–762	The first plague pandemic in Europe.
700s	Leprosy first emerges in Europe.
c. 900	Salerno medical school is founded.
c. 900	The Arab physician Rhases identifies and describes various infectious diseases, including plague, consumption, and smallpox.
c. 950–1347	Europe enjoys a period relatively free of infectious diseases.
c. 1010	Avicenna writes his *Canon*, which is to have a major influence on European medicine for the next eight hundred years.
1150	Bologna medical school is founded.
1168	Oxford University is founded.
1200	Paris University is founded.
1250	Climate changes cause a drop in food productivity in Europe.
1260s	Human dissections are first carried out at Bologna.
1275	William of Saliceto provides earliest record of a human dissection in his *Surgery*.
1289	Montpellier University is founded.
1300–1320s	Henri de Mondeville works as a surgeon and anatomist at Montpellier University.
1300–1330	Bubonic plague spreads from Mongolia.
1315–1320	Outbreaks of famine in Europe.
1347–1352	The Black Death wipes out about a third of Europe's population.
1353	Boccaccio writes *The Decameron*.
1361–1362	The plague kills between 10 and 20 percent of Europe's population.
1363	Guy de Chauliac publishes *Chirurgia Magna*.
1369	A third outbreak of bubonic plague kills a further 10–15 percent of Europe's population.
1381	The English Peasants' Revolt.
1400	Leprosy virtually disappears in Europe.
c. 1440	Gutenberg invents printing press.
1492	Columbus discovers the New World.

For Further Research

Books to Read

Phyllis Corzine and Robert Steven Gottfried, *The Black Death*. San Diego: Greenhaven Press, 1997.

Tracee de Hahn, *The Black Death*. Bromall, PA: Chelsea House, 2001.

Kathryn Hinds, *Life in the Middle Ages*. Salt Lake City, UT: Benchmark Books, 2000.

Andrew Langley, *DK Eyewitness Guides: Medieval Life*. London: Dorling Kindersley, 1996.

Earle Rice, *Life in the Middle Ages*. San Diego, CA: Lucent Books, 1998.

Works Consulted

Giovanni Boccaccio, *The Decameron*. Translated by Frances Winwar. New York: Modern Library, 1955.

Carlo Cipolla, *Public Health and the Medical Profession in the Renaissance*. Cambridge, UK: Cambridge University Press, 1976.

H.B. Dewing, ed., *History of the Wars*. New York: Macmillan, 1914.

Michael Dols, *The Black Death in the Middle East*. Princeton, NJ: Princeton University Press, 1977.

John Fordun, *Chronicle*. Edited by W.F. Skene. Edinburgh: Edmonston and Douglass, 1880.

Jean de Froissart, *Chronicles*. Edited by Geoffrey Brereton. New York: Penguin Books, 1968.

J. Gairdner, ed., *The Paston Letters*. London. Chatto & Windus, 1904.

John Lydgate, *Lydgate's Minor Poems*. Edited by H.N. MacCracken. Oxford: Early English Text Society, 1933.

Maxwell-Lyte HC, ed., *The Register of Thomas Bekynton, Bishop of Bath and Wells 1443–1465*. Somerset, UK: Somerset Record Society, 1934.

A.R. Myers, *English Historical Documents*. London: Eyre & Spo, 1969.

Henri de Mondeville, *Surgery* [*Chirurgie*]. Edited by E. Nicaise. Paris: Félix Alcan, 1893.

Johannes de Trokelowe, *Annates*. Edited by H.T. Riley. Translated by Brian Tierney. London: Rolls Series, 1866.

Hildegard von Bingen, *Physica*. Translated from Latin by Priscilla Throop. Rochester, VT: Healing Arts Press, 1998.

Glossary

abbess Nun in charge of a convent.

anatomy The internal structure of a human or animal.

anointment The application of oil or ointment on someone's head and feet as part of a religious ceremony.

antiseptics Remedies that prevent or reduce infection by killing harmful bacteria.

bacteria The microorganisms (tiny living things) responsible for many diseases.

bile A yellowish green fluid produced by the liver.

buboes Swellings, especially in the area of the armpits or groin, suffered by victims of the plague.

Byzantine The Byzantine Empire began as the eastern part of the late Roman Empire with Constantinople (modern Istanbul) as its capital. It lasted from 395 to 1453 A.D.

caravan A group of traders, especially in Africa and Asia, traveling together for safety, usually with a train of camels.

cautery Sealing a wound or destroying infected tissue by burning.

cholera An acute, often fatal disease caused by eating food or drinking water infected by the cholera bacterium.

clerics Men qualified to give religious services in the Church.

conjunction Simultaneous occurrence of events.

contagious Transmittable from one person or animal to another, either by direct contact, such as touching an infected person, or by indirect contact.

convents Communities of women whose lives are devoted to religious worship.

cupping A partial vacuum is created inside a glass container by heat or suction, and this is applied to a patient's skin to increase the blood supply in the tissues below.

death masks Casts made of someone's face after death.

decomposition The breaking down of organic matter, including human corpses, through the action of fungi and bacteria.

diagnosis The identifying of an illness.

diphtheria A serious infectious disease that attacks the throat, the heart, and the nervous system.

dissection The cutting up of a body for study.

dormant In an inactive state.

dysentery A disease of the lower intestine, causing fever, diarrhea containing blood, and stomach cramps.

epidemic A rapid and widespread outbreak of a disease.

friars Members of any of several religious orders. Friars were forbidden to own property, and were encouraged to work or beg for a living.

hemlock A poisonous herb of the carrot family with small white flowers.

henbane A poisonous plant of the nightshade family with hairy, sticky leaves and an unpleasant smell.

malnutrition A lack of healthy foods in the diet which leads to physical harm.

monastery A community of men, especially monks, living together and observing religious vows.

Mongol A member of the nomadic peoples who inhabited Mongolia and established the Mongol Empire in the thirteenth century.

nobility A high-ranking class of people in a country, who achieved their status through birth.

nomadic Relating to groups of people who move from place to place seasonally in search of pasture for their herds or food and water.

nutrition The process of absorbing the nourishing substances from food in order to keep healthy or to grow.

peasantry A class of poor people who are usually dependent on farming the land for all their food.

phlegm Thick mucus secreted from the walls of the respiratory passages, especially when suffering from a cold. In medieval medicine, phlegm was one of the four humors and was believed to be cold and moist in nature, causing sluggishness and apathy.

pogroms Campaigns of persecution or extermination directed against an ethnic group, especially Jews.

postmortems Examinations of corpses to establish the cause of death.

resurrection The rising of the dead on Judgment Day, as anticipated by Christians, Jews, and Muslims.

salvation In the Christian religion, this means the saving of oneself from the consequences of sin through prayer or good deeds.

typhoid A serious, sometimes fatal, infection of the digestive system caused by eating food or drinking water contaminated with *Salmonella typhi*.

Yersina pestis The bacteria that causes plague.

Index